Puffin Books

Professor Branestawm's Pocket Motor Car

Professor Branestawm's genius for invention is at its most wonderful in the two stories in this book, specially written for younger admirers of the great inventor.

In the first story, he decides to solve Great Pagwell's parking problems by making an inflatable motor car. And in the second, he creates a highly ingenious machine that will write all those letters he can't be bothered to write himself. But, as with all of the professor's inventions, nothing goes quite as well as it should . . .

Professor Branestawm has been delighting children for many years with his fun and foolery. This delightful book, with its large print and many pictures, will make him available to a younger, but equally appreciative, audience.

Norman Hunter was born in London in 1899. He lived in Johannesburg for twenty years but now lives in England near the Thames.

Other books by Norman Hunter

NORMAN HUNTER

Professor Branestawm's Pocket Motor Car

Illustrated by Gerald Rose

PUFFIN BOOKS

PUFFIN BOOKS

Published by the Penguin Group
Penguin Books Ltd, 27 Wrights Lane, London W8 5TZ, England
Penguin Books USA Inc., 375 Hudson Street, New York, New York 10014, USA
Penguin Books Australia Ltd, Ringwood, Victoria, Australia
Penguin Books Canada Ltd, 10 Alcorn Avenue, Toronto, Ontario, Canada M4V 3B2
Penguin Books (NZ) Ltd, 182–190 Wairau Road, Auckland 10, New Zealand

Penguin Books Ltd, Registered Offices: Harmondsworth, Middlesex, England

Professor Branestawm's Pocket Motor Car first published by The Bodley Head 1981
Professor Branestawm and the Wild Letters first published by The Bodley Head 1981
Published in one volume in Puffin Books 1982
10 9 8

Printed in England by Clays Ltd, St Ives plc
Filmset in Monophoto Plantin

Contents

Professor Branestawm's
Pocket Motor Car

The people of Great Pagwell will never forget the day it rained doughnuts and jam tarts in the High Street.

It was all due to Professor Branestawm's marvellous and astonishing pocket motor car.

But how can folding motor cars cause showers of cakes in high streets? Very strange. Most not-understandable. Ha!

'You, um, ah, see,' said Professor Branestawm, stuffing three pairs of spectacles into his pocket and putting the other two pairs on top of his head, 'the trouble with motor cars is that one, um, ah, cannot always find somewhere to park them.'

'Ha, my word, by Jove, yes!' said his friend, Colonel Dedshott, who always rode a horse and was never bothered with parking problems because there aren't any notices that say 'No horse-parking'.

'My invention,' went on the Professor, 'does away with all that.' He waved his hand towards a motor car that looked like a raspberry blancmange with lemon-flavoured wheels.

'This car,' said the Professor, 'is made like those little boats and Li-los that you blow up. When I arrive where I want to be, I just, um, ah, do this.' He turned a button on the car. It went *hissssssss*, *zimmy*, *zim*,

gradually collapsed and then went flat. The Professor folded it, rolled it up and put it in his pocket.

'No parking problems,' he said. 'And what is, um, ah, more, it needs no petrol.'

'How does it go then?' asked the Mayor of Pagwell.

'It goes by pumped-up air,' said the Professor. 'You just pump it up like a bicycle tyre and the pumped-up air drives it along. When the car begins to lose some of its air, you simply stop at a garage where they pump it up for you again, just as they pump up motor car tyres.'

'Marvellous, what,' said Commander

Hardaport (Retired). 'Ought to invent folding battleship like that, y'know.'

The Professor took the folded car out of his pocket, pumped it up, got in, and the car and the Professor slid away up the street.

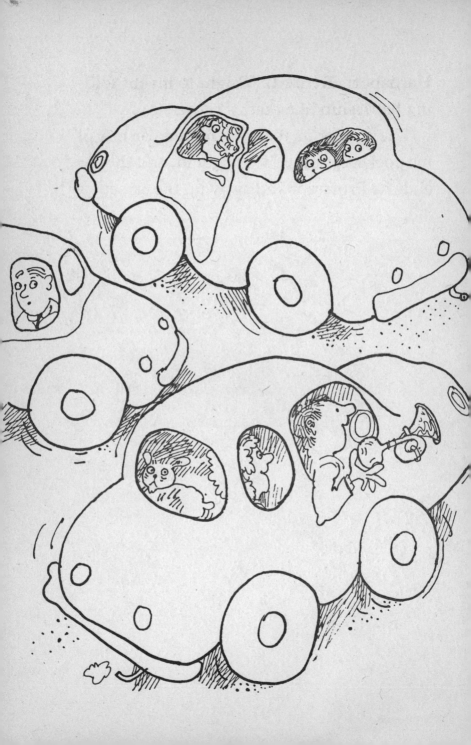

Professor Branestawm's folding pocket motor car was the talk of Pagwell. All the Councillors wanted one. So did the Headmaster of Pagwell College and several of the shopkeepers. The Vicar would have liked one too, as it would have been easier to ride than his bicycle.

'I do think it's nice, sir, your invention being so popular,' said Mrs Flittersnoop, the Professor's housekeeper, handing him a piece of currant cake, which he stirred his tea with and tried to eat the spoon.

'Um, ah, yes,' he said. 'I must get busy making pocket motor cars for everyone,' and he went into his inventory, accompanied by the tablecloth which he had stuffed into his pocket in mistake for his handkerchief.

Soon the streets of Pagwell were full of bouncing, noiseless, smell-free, folding plastic motor cars. In fact about the only noise in the streets came from police cars rushing around trying to find someone

parked in a forbidden place. But nobody was parked anywhere. Instead, people were walking about with their pockets bulging with the Professor's wonderful folding motor cars.

'My invention has other benefits,' said the Professor to Mrs Flittersnoop one breakfast time. 'If you pumped it up with, um, er, special gas, it would float like a balloon and you could fly above the crowded roads. And if you should accidentally run into something in one of my folding pumped-up cars, it will simply bounce off and no, um, er, harm done.'

'Yes, indeed, I'm sure, sir,' said Mrs Flittersnoop, who was always careful not to run into anything and was also careful not to run out of anything, such as sugar, or fancy biscuits, or Wizard Instant Jelly Powder at 2p off if you bought more than you wanted.

'Or,' continued the Professor, 'if you should accidentally drive off a bridge and into the water, this car would not sink, and if you fancied a trip to France, you would not need to take a boat.'

Nearly everybody was delighted with the Professor's invention. Nearly everybody that is, except the car park people, who rather hated seeing their lovely car parks empty, and the traffic wardens who were stamping around with books of gorgeous tickets and no cars to slap them on. And the petrol station people got ever so slightly cheesed off giving out air for nothing instead of petrol at goodness knows how much a gallon.

But Mrs Flittersnoop was as delighted as if she'd found a long-lost recipe for rhubarb surprise.

'It's high time your talents were recognized, sir,' she said, screwing back her hair a bit tighter to show she meant what she was saying. 'It's wonderful that your new motor car is such a success.'

'Er, um, ah, yes,' muttered the Professor. 'But I wish you wouldn't keep saying that, Mrs, er, Flittersnoop. I can't help feeling all this praise and success may lead to something going wrong.'

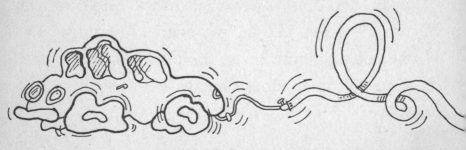

'Oh, but nothing
can go wrong this
time, sir,' said
Mrs Flittersnoop.
    Oh dear! Why did
she have to say that?
A Branestawm
disaster was just
combing its hair
and getting ready
to happen.

It was a nice sunny Tuesday morning. The High Street was full of the Professor's wonderful motor cars and vans going silently up and down, and with people with bulging pockets where they'd parked the Professor's wonderful folding vehicles.

The Professor himself, in his own folding motor car, slid noiselessly to a stop outside the ironmonger's, let the air out of his car, folded it up and stuffed it into his pocket, which it went only half-way into as the pocket was already half-full of bits of wood and cardboard and wire for making inventions.

Then he went into the ironmonger's and bought a bag of nice sharp nails for mending a fence in the garden that a rather wild sunflower had pulled down.

He came out of the shop, went to the kerb, waited for the pedestrian light to go green, then, as *pip, pip, pip, pip*, sounded as a sign that people could cross the road safely, he stepped out. But he was so taken up with thinking of a new invention for a typewriter

that always spelt words correctly even if you didn't, that he was only half-way across the road when the pips stopped and the lights began flashing to tell him he ought to be all the way across.

'Dear me, I, um, ah,' he muttered. He tried to hurry, dropped his umbrella, picked it up and dropped the bag of nails, dashed across to the kerb just as the lights went red for pedestrians and green for traffic.

The cars and vans surged forward.

But, oh calamity! One of the vans ran over the Professor's bag of sharp nails.

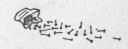

And, oh worse calamity! It was a van belonging to the Pagwell Bakery. And tut, tut, oh, wow! It was one of the Professor's special folding, pumped-up motor cars made as a van. And oh, oh, still more oh! It was full of cakes of all kinds.

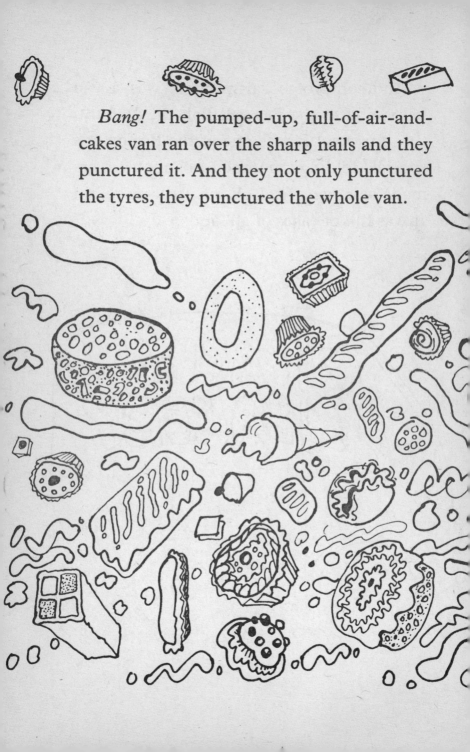

Bang! The pumped-up, full-of-air-and-cakes van ran over the sharp nails and they punctured it. And they not only punctured the tyres, they punctured the whole van.

There was the very great-grandfather of a bang. The whole van burst into bits. Doughnuts, jam tarts, assorted pastries of the best quality shot up into the air and rained down all over the High Street. Shoppers were smothered in lovely cakes that weren't on their shopping lists.

The Vicar of Pagwell was hit by a flying angel cake. A rum baba struck Commander Hardaport (Retired) amidships, and policemen, running up blowing their whistles, were heavily outnumbered by bouncing buns, mad macaroons and scampering scones.

'Oh, um, ah, dear me!' muttered the Professor, dodging a descending doughnut. 'This is most, um, ah . . .'

Then there was a mad scramble and soon
all the escaping cakes were gathered up and
taken home by joyful shoppers while policemen, traffic wardens and Professor Branestawm, helped by Colonel Dedshott and his
Catapult Cavaliers, got the place tidied up a
bit.

'I, um, ah, fear my wonderful invention turned out to be a disaster,' groaned the Professor.

But it wasn't altogether a disaster. Not for the Pagwell Bakery. The loss of their folding pocket van was more than made up for by the rush of customers, because people who had never tasted their cakes before found the ones they had caught in the High Street shower were so delicious they wanted more.

But it was the end

of Professor Branestawm's folding pocket
motor car,

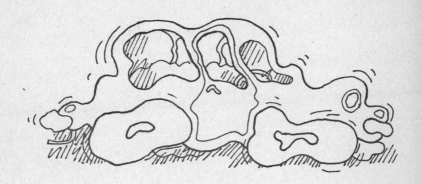

which was a pity.

Professor Branestawm
and the Wild Letters

Scratch, scratch. Squeak, squeak. Crumple, crumple. Plonk.

No, it wasn't a Branestawm invention doing its thing. It was the Professor in his dining-room, writing letters, crumpling them up, throwing them away and starting again.

Scratch, scratch, squeak.

Then Mrs Flittersnoop, the Professor's housekeeper, came in with a pot of tea and home-made cakes of her own invention.

'This, um, ah, letter-writing can be most, er, ah,' said the Professor, polishing his spectacles with one of Mrs Flittersnoop's sponge cakes.

'Yes, indeed, I'm sure, sir,' said Mrs Flittersnoop.

'It takes so much time and keeps me from inventing,' said the Professor. 'What with thank you letters for birthday and Christmas presents. My, um, ah, birthday comes so near Christmas that I get a lot of presents all at once and so have a lot of letters to write.'

'Very nice, I'm sure, sir,' said Mrs Flittersnoop, who liked getting presents if they were boxes of chocolates, but not if they were warm, woolly vests that she couldn't wear because they tickled.

'Of course,' said the Professor, stirring his tea with two of his five pairs of spectacles, 'the shops have a lot of cards that say "Thank You" and "Get Well" and "Happy Birthday", but they don't seem very, ah, suitable sometimes. I could hardly send a card to Pagwell Council complaining about the dustmen not calling, which said, "Many Happy Returns", if they hadn't returned to collect the rubbish.'

Mrs Flittersnoop cleared away the tea things and went to see about some ironing, while the Professor went on writing letters and wishing he needn't.

Suddenly he had an idea. Right out of nowhere it came. Like catching the measles, only nicer.

'Why shouldn't I invent a machine that writes letters?' he thought to himself. And as he couldn't think of any reason why he shouldn't, he did.

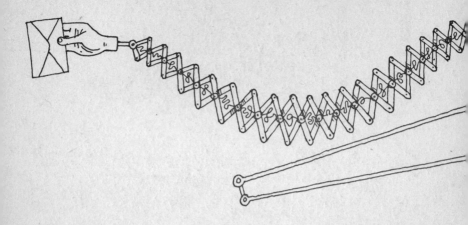

Professor Branestawm's marvellous letter-writing machine was finished. It had taken some doing, but it was done. It looked like three and a half typewriters, two television sets with no screens, a bent egg whisk and several empty jam jars. It was simply smothered in knobs and littered with levers, and it had places for letter paper and envelopes, and even for postcards, if you wanted it to send them.

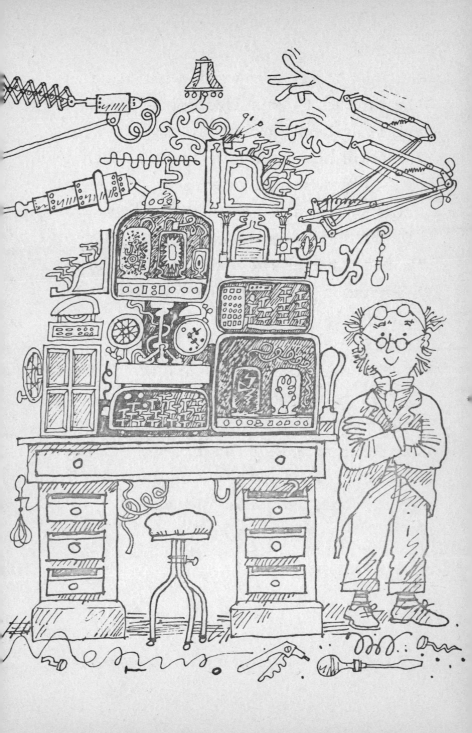

'Jolly clever, my word, what!' said his best friend, Colonel Dedshott of the Catapult Cavaliers, when he saw it.

'I will now show you how the machine works by writing a letter asking you to tea next Wednesday, Dedshott,' said the Professor. 'I first move this pointer to your name. Then I press the button marked "invitation" and the one marked "tea". Then I dial it for next Wednesday and pull this lever.'

He pulled the lever. The machine went *gurgle gurgle, whizzy wiz, buzzy buz, pop bing clank*. Then a neatly typed letter, ready folded in an envelope addressed to Colonel Dedshott, shot out of the machine and hit the Colonel right on his medals.

In two seconds the Colonel had it opened and read out, 'Dear Dedshott, will you come to tea with me next Wednesday? Yours, Branestawm.'

'By Jove, wish you'd make me a machine for writing my military reports!' said the Colonel.

'Unfortunately,' said the Professor, 'this machine took so long to make that I couldn't possibly make another one.'

'Dear me,' said the Vicar of Pagwell, who had come to see if the machine could write sermons for him. 'One of these machines would be most useful to me.'

'Well, um, ah,' said the Professor, waving spectacles about, 'I can't make you both special machines, but you are welcome to come here and use this one.'

'That is most kind,' said the Vicar. 'But I think we should arrange which day each of us can come to use it, so that we do not get in one another's way.'

'Ho, no problem for me,' grunted the Colonel. 'Couldn't use the machine in your

house anyway, Branestawm. Military reports most hush-hush. Wouldn't do.'

So it was finally arranged that the Vicar could come and use the letter-writing machine on Tuesdays. The Mayor, who also wanted to use it when he heard about it, could come on Thursdays. Doctor Mumpzanmeazle preferred Fridays and Miss Frenzie of the Pagwell Book Publishing Company said Mondays would suit her best as it was her secretary, Violet's, day off.

After that the visitors said thank you very much and left, leaving the Professor to think about all the letters he had to write.

The machine had these written and posted for him in less time than it took Mrs Flittersnoop to make two cups of instant coffee. This, in fact, took rather a lot of instants, as the Professor had taken the jar of instant coffee to try to invent a way of

making orange jam without it turning into
marmalade.

Professor Branestawm's letter-writing machine was a huge success. It even had an arrangement for posting the letters in the box just outside the Professor's house.

The Professor was so pleased with it that he used it to write letters to everyone he could think of. Thank you letters rained on people who had given the Professor presents.

Get well cards arrived for
people with the slightest
cold or tummy-ache,

and Pagwell Council were nearly
buried in letters of complaint from the
Professor about smelly drains, the
roads, the rates and the weather.

70

The Vicar sent off encouraging letters to get people to come to church as often as possible.

Miss Frenzie sent flocks of letters about her books on cooking that does itself, or how to make your pocket-money go further.

And Doctor Mumpzan-meazle had a lovely time writing medical letters.

BAD CASE OF PULLED LEG

Then the Mayor did it. In fact he did it twice.

First he came on a Wednesday instead of a Thursday and that upset Mr Hokkibats who was there writing cricket letters. Then he tried to use the machine to write a letter to the Professor complaining about the letters of complaint the Professor had sent to Pagwell Council.

That really did it. No Branestawm invention was going to have the Professor complained to about something he'd complained about. No, jolly well, fear.

It sent the Mayor a letter telling him if he had complaints he should go to the hospital.

The Mayor was furious. He kicked the machine in a highly mechanical part.

Bang! Pwouff! Buzzzzzzz, boom!

A cloud of smoke poured out of the machine, and the Mayor shot out of the house just in time to be missed by a volley of letters refusing to pay the rates.

Then the machine
really got going.

It sent a letter to
the Vicar telling him
to climb up on his
own steeple.

It wrote to Doctor
Mumpzanmeazle
saying 'get spotted'.

It instructed the gas company to blow up

and the electricity people to get switched off.

But oh, most terrible thing. Every one of these rude letters had been written on Professor Branestawm's own letter paper which had his address printed at the top, so people naturally thought they came from the Professor.

'All that inventing must have gone to the chap's head,' grunted General Shatterfortz, who'd had an urgent despatch from the machine telling him to form fours and march to April.

'I really fear the Professor has been overworking,' murmured the Vicar, looking at a letter advising him to sing hymn number 54675867655344B.

Then Colonel Dedshott got a letter saying, 'Stand to attention and jump in the lake!'

'My word, by Jove!' cried the Colonel when he read it. 'Can't be from Branestawm. Never write *me* a letter like that. Must be mischief afoot.'

Collecting up his Catapult Cavaliers on the way he dashed round to the Professor's house. Outside there was a crowd of people, shouting and waving letters the machine had sent them.

'Down with Branestawm!' they were yelling. 'We won't be written to like that! Never been so insulted in our lives.'

'Make way!' shouted the Colonel, drawing his sword and chopping a long feather off Mrs Trumpington-Smawl's hat. This didn't make her any angrier than she was

before, because it couldn't, since she was already ten times wild about a letter she'd received calling her an old what's-its-name.

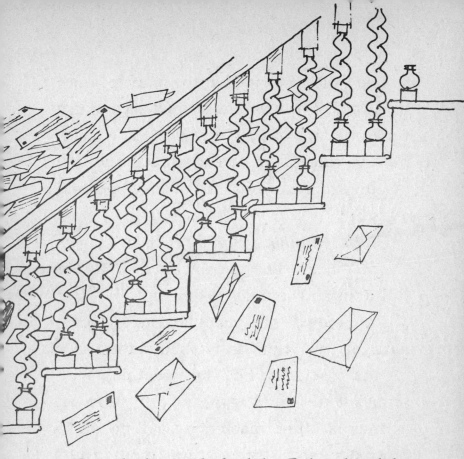

Into the house dashed the Colonel and the Catapult Cavaliers, followed by as many of the crowd as could get in, which was hardly any.

The machine met them with a shower of postcards saying, 'Having a lovely time. Wish you weren't here.'

The Colonel swiped at the machine with his sword. The machine swiped back with a rude postcard of Brighton Pier. The Catapult Cavaliers counter-attacked, and the machine replied with a hail of envelopes and a gas bill.

Crash. Wallop. Bongetty bong. Boom. Crackle buzzz. The machine fired a volley of full stops and commas.

The crowd stopped shouting, 'Down with the Professor!' and joined in the attack on the machine. The air was thick with airmail letters and invitations to buzz off and scram. The machine's spelling broke down under the strain. It poured out insults nobody could understand.

87

Bang, crash, the Catapult Cavaliers went at it with Mrs Flittersnoop's best frying-pan that they'd fetched from the kitchen. The machine spat severe sentences at them. *Bang. Crash. Poppety blank boom.*

Then out from under the sideboard, where he'd been hiding for safety, crawled the Professor. He hit the machine in just the right place with a special hammer he happened to have with him.

Bangetty, crash. Zoom, bong, bash.

The frightful letter-writing machine collapsed with a crash of words and exclamation marks. It had been defeated just in time to stop it writing a ticking-off letter to the Queen. Thank goodness for that.

'If only people would leave my inventions alone,' said the Professor to Mrs Flittersnoop later on, after a good strong cup of tea and strengthening scones, 'there would be no trouble. Now I shall have to write my own letters again.'

'Yes, indeed, I'm sure, sir,' said Mrs
Flittersnoop, feeling thankful another attack
of inventions was over.

Also in Young Puffin

Dragonrise

Kathryn Cave

What do dragons like to eat best?

When the dragon Tom found under his bed told him the answer, Tom began to worry. Although he offered his new friend all sorts of tasty morsels as a substitute, the dragon just didn't seem to be interested. Then Tom's elder sister, Sarah, did something that Tom could not forgive – and he realized that the dragon could help him take an unusual revenge!